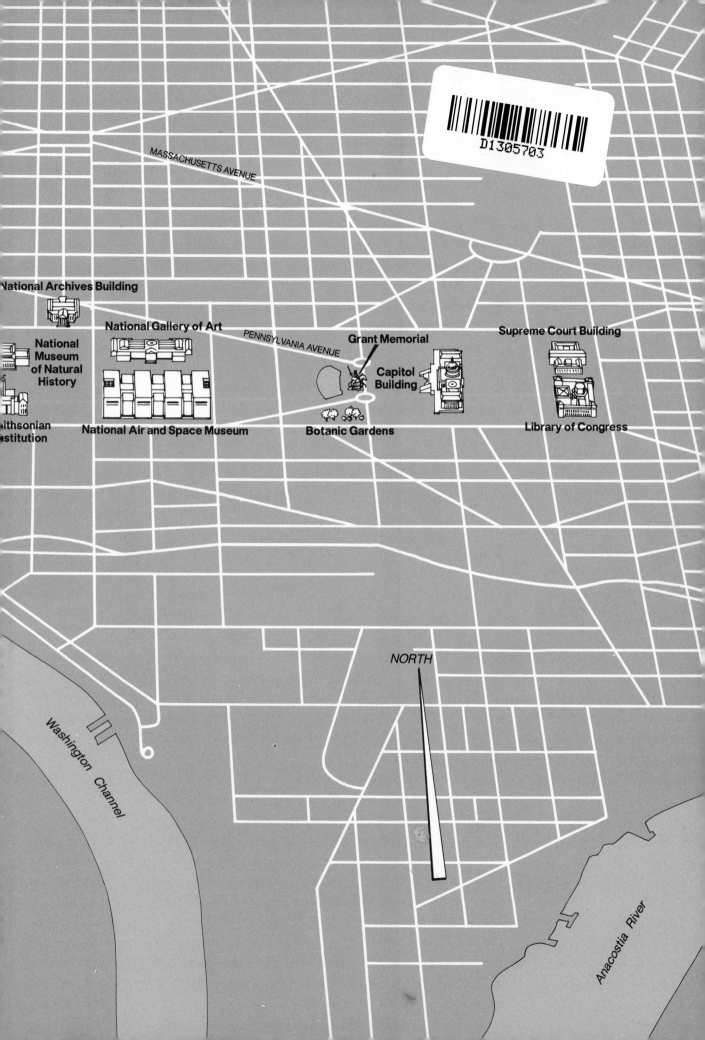

A Visit to
Washington, D.C.

By Jill Krementz

SCHOLASTIC INC./New York

Also by Jill Krementz

The Face of South Vietnam
(with text by Dean Brelis)

Sweet Pea—A Black Girl
Growing Up in the Rural South

Words and Their Masters
(with text by Israel Shenker)

A Very Young Dancer

A Very Young Rider

A Very Young Gymnast

A Very Young Circus Flyer

A Very Young Skater

The Writer's Image

How It Feels When a Parent Dies

How It Feels to be Adopted

How It Feels When Parents Divorce

The Fun of Cooking

Lily Goes to the Playground

Jack Goes to the Beach

Taryn Goes to the Dentist

Benjy Goes to a Restaurant

Katherine Goes to Nursery School

Jamie Goes on an Airplane

Zachary Goes to the Zoo

Holly's Farm Animals

Photograph of Ling-Ling and Hsing-Hsing by Jessie Cohen.
Reprinted courtesy of the Office of Graphics and Exhibits,
National Zoological Park

Copyright © 1987 by Jill Krementz.
All rights reserved. Published by Scholastic Inc.
SCHOLASTIC HARDCOVER is a trademark of Scholastic Inc.
Endpaper map by Paul Pugliese.

Library of Congress Cataloging-in-Publication Data

Krementz, Jill.
A visit to Washington, D.C.

(Scholastic hardcover)
Summary: Text and photographs feature Matt
Wilson, age six, who introduces the sights of
his beautiful and interesting hometown, Washington, D.C.
1. Washington (D.C.)—Juvenile literature.
2. Washington (D.C.)—Description—1981-
Guide-books—Juvenile literature. [1. Washington
(D.C.)—Description] I. Title. II Title:
Visit to Washington, D.C.
F194.3.K74   1987   917.53'044   86-27973

ISBN 0-590-40582-9

12 11 10 9 8 7 6 5 4 3 2 1   7 8 9/8 0 1 2/9

Printed in the U.S.A.   23

First Scholastic printing, May 1987

*This book is dedicated
to
Chris Downey,
with much love.*

My name's Matt Wilson, and I'm six years old. I live in Washington, D.C. That's the Capitol building behind me. It's where the members of Congress make the laws. Most of the U.S. government is in Washington. The city was named for General George Washington, who was the first President of our country.

One of the best things about living in Washington is that
I've learned so much about the history of our country.

My whole family enjoys sightseeing—Daddy, Mommy,
and my little brother Cole.

There are lots of monuments to Presidents, like the one to Thomas Jefferson. It's fun to look at it from up in the cherry trees. They're very good for climbing.

In the spring, people come to Washington to see the trees' pink blossoms, which only last a few weeks. They were given to America by the Japanese.

One statue perfect for climbing is the one of Albert Einstein.
He was a famous scientist who changed the way we think
about the universe.

Sometimes I whisper a secret in his ear.

On the west front of the Capitol building is another great climbing statue of soldiers fighting in the Civil War. It's called the Grant Memorial.

I like to sit on a horse and yell, "Charge!"

Some monuments honor soldiers who fought and died for America. At the Vietnam Memorial there is a list on shining black granite of all the men and women who were lost in that war.

Daddy's older brother died in Vietnam, so this is a very special place for our family to visit.

My dad always likes to touch my uncle's name with his fingers.

Sometimes people leave flowers at the foot of the wall.

There's a statue at the Vietnam Memorial, too. It's of three soldiers
like my uncle, and they look very real.

If you go behind them you can see their canteens
and the bullets they had to carry.

My dad says sometimes we don't know the names of all the soldiers who died. At Arlington Cemetery there is a memorial for them, too. It's called the Tomb of the Unknown Soldier.

They have a changing of the guard every half hour. When this happens, all the visitors are told to "stand and remain silent."

The soldiers are very good at shining their shoes, polishing their brass, and cleaning their guns. Their blue uniforms are called "blues."

Their shoes have "cheaters" on them, which make a really loud noise when they click their heels together.

When the bugler plays taps everybody stands up very straight.
It makes me feel proud of my country.

One time I got to shake hands with him.

One of the nicest places in Washington is the Botanic Gardens.
It's like being in an indoor jungle.

My favorite flowers
are the orchids. They
smell wonderful.

There are all kinds of
exotic plants with names
like "Painted Lady."

NEOREGELIA HYBRID CV.
PAINTED LADY
BROMELIACEAE

I never knew there were so many sizes and shapes of cactus plants.
But they all have one thing in common: They're prickly!

One cactus is so tall they cut a hole in the roof to let it out.

Sometimes we feed the ducks at the Reflecting Pool. It reflects the Washington Monument, named after George Washington.

The monument has flags all the way around it. You can ride to the top in an elevator and sometimes they let you walk down the 898 steps.

Cole and I play in the fields nearby. In the spring when the daffodils are in bloom, we have to be careful not to step on them.

The mall's a big lawn in the middle of all the monuments, and the merry-go-round there is definitely worth a visit.

Near the merry-go-round, in the National Museum of Natural History,
is one of our favorite places—the Discovery Room. It's called that
because you can explore and discover lots of things there.

One wall has boxes full of things like Indian dolls, animal skulls,
bark from trees, coral from the ocean, spices, sea urchin shells, and frogs.

It's such a relaxing place that lots of the grown-ups call it the "Recovery Room."

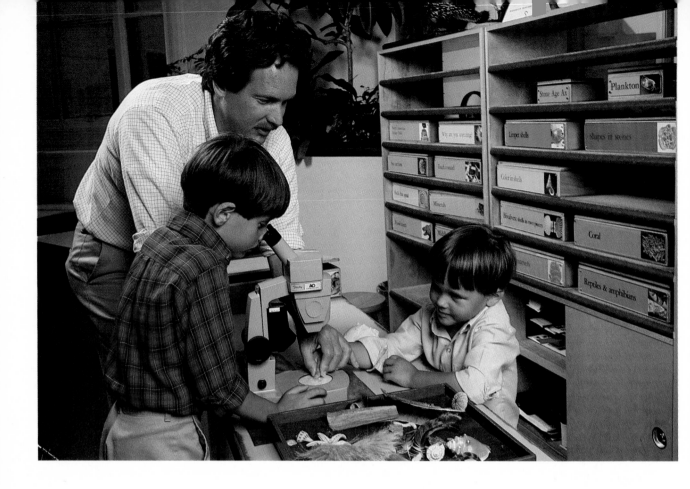

You can look at and touch everything, including a microscope anyone can use. Cole's fingernail looked really weird!

In one corner they have a collection of costumes you can try on. They're from many different countries. The Indian gloves have cuffs that are decorated with tiny beads. The moccasins smell like smoke because they're made from smoked moose hide.

It's a great place to meet other kids. Or a crocodile!

We explore at the Air and Space Museum, too. I love this place because it's full of airplanes, rockets, missiles, and space capsules. They even have the suits that our astronauts wore when they were in space.

I also like the suits of armor
that knights wore in medieval
times.

In the workshop at the Washington
Cathedral you can make a brass
rubbing of a knight in armor with
crayons made from beeswax.

I made a rubbing of Edward,
the Black Prince.

If you like money, be sure to visit the Bureau of Engraving and Printing! Dollar bills—ones, fives, tens, twenties, fifties, and hundreds—all come off the printing presses in big sheets. Then they're checked for mistakes before they are cut into single bills.

I learned a lot about our currency. All bills say "In God We Trust" on them and they aren't made out of paper. They're made of 75 percent cotton and 25 percent linen, which is why they last so long. Paper money would only last a week!

The Bureau of Engraving and Printing makes about 6.2 billion dollar bills a year. The ink on them never completely dries. If you rub a bill on a piece of white paper with your thumbnail, the ink will come off.

Andrew Jackson is on the twenty dollar bill. Do you know which bill George Washington is on?

The National Gallery of Art has another picture of George Washington. Mom said he's not smiling because he had wooden teeth, which didn't fit very well. She asked me if I'd like to wear a powdered wig with a little bow.

I said, "No way!"

The reason there are so many presidential monuments and statues
in Washington is because most of the Presidents lived in this city.

The White House was built in 1792. John Adams, our second President,
moved there in 1800, and that's where all the Presidents have lived ever since.
You can take guided tours through the White House during special hours.

Thomas Jefferson was our third President, and he was also a famous architect. His monument looks like the kind of houses he used to build.

The huge statue of Jefferson inside the monument is Cole's favorite.

At the Lincoln Memorial there's a gigantic statue of Abraham Lincoln sitting in a chair. I learned about him at school. He was the 16th President and he stopped slavery.

President John F. Kennedy's grave has a flame that never goes out so we'll always remember him. It's called the Eternal Flame. I asked my dad what keeps the fire burning all the time. He said it's oil. At night the flame is especially pretty.

AND SO MY FELLOW AMERICANS
ASK NOT WHAT YOUR COUNTRY CAN DO FOR YOU
ASK WHAT YOU CAN DO FOR YOUR COUNTRY
MY FELLOW CITIZENS OF THE WORLD · ASK NOT
WHAT AMERICA WILL DO FOR YOU · BUT WHAT TOGETHER
WE CAN DO FOR THE FREEDOM OF MAN

President Kennedy's most famous sayings
are set in stone nearby.

The Eternal Flame is at Arlington Cemetery. Lots of generals and other important people are buried there. It's actually in Virginia on a beautiful hill that overlooks the Potomac River and Washington on the other side.

If you come to Washington during the summer, be sure to end the day with a visit to the Capitol grounds where you can listen to a military band and watch the sun set. Sometimes we bring a picnic supper.

There are so many exciting things to see and do in Washington, D.C.
If I tried to tell you about all of them, this book would be a million pages long.
I've told you about some of our favorite places!

There are maps everywhere, which make it easy to find other museums
and monuments. Or you might want to visit the pandas from China at the
National Zoo or see the old railway cars at the Museum of American History.

Don't forget your camera. I know you'll have a great time!

MADISON COUNTY
~~ION PUBLIC LIBRARY SYSTEM~~
CANTON, MISS. 39046

Capitol Building
Capitol Hill
(202) 225-6827
Guided tours daily,
9:00 A.M.-3:45 P.M.
Closed Thanksgiving, Christmas Day, and
New Year's Day

Jefferson Memorial
South Bank, Tidal Basin
(202) 426-6841
Daily, 8:00 A.M.-Midnight
Japanese Cherry Trees
Tidal Basin

Albert Einstein Statue
Outside of National Academy of Sciences
22nd Street and Constitution Avenue, NW

The Grant Memorial
West Front, Capitol Building

Vietnam Memorial
Mall, near 23rd Street, NW
(202) 426-6841
Daily, 8:00 A.M.-Midnight

Tomb of the Unknown Soldier
Arlington Cemetery
Arlington, VA
(703) 692-0931
Daily, 8:00 A.M.-5:00 P.M.
Changing of the guard every hour; every
half hour during the summer.

Botanic Gardens
Maryland Avenue, between 1st and 2nd
Streets, SW
(202) 225-7099
Open daily, 9:00 A.M.-5:00 P.M.

Washington Monument, Reflecting Pool
Mall at 15th Street, NW
(202) 426-6841
Daily, March 20-Labor Day, 8:00 A.M.-Midnight
Day after Labor Day-March 19, 9:00 A.M.-
5:00 P.M.

Carousel
Mall, across from Arts & Industries Building
A Smithsonian Museum
900 Jefferson Drive, SW
(703) 560-2846
May-Aug., M-F, 10:00 A.M.-4:30 P.M.
Sat & Sun, 10:00 A.M.-5:30 P.M.
Sept., open weekends only
Closed Oct.-May 1st

Discovery Room
National Museum of Natural History
A Smithsonian Museum
10th Street and Constitution Avenue, NW
(202) 357-2695
M-Th, 12:00 P.M.-2:30 P.M.
F-Sun, 10:30 A.M.-3:30 P.M.

The National Air and Space Museum
A Smithsonian Museum
7th Street and Independence Avenue, SW
(202) 357-2020, 357-2700
Open daily, 10:00 A.M.-5:30 P.M.
Closed Christmas Day

Brass rubbing workshop
Washington National Cathedral
Wisconsin and Massachusetts Avenues, NW
(202) 364-0030
Workshop open daily, 9:30 A.M.-5:00 P.M.
Fee for rubbings from $2-$20

Bureau of Engraving and Printing
14th and C Streets, SW
(202) 566-2000
M-F, 9:00 A.M.-2:00 P.M.
Closed legal holidays

National Gallery of Art
A Smithsonian Museum
6th Street and Constitution Avenue, NW
(202) 842-6191
M-Sat, 10:00 A.M.-5:00 P.M.
Sun, 12:00 P.M.-9:00 P.M.
Closed Christmas Day and New Year's Day

The White House
1600 Pennsylvania Avenue, NW
(202) 456-2200
Guided tours, Tues.-Sat., 10:00 A.M.-12:00 P.M.

Lincoln Memorial
West Potomac Park, foot of 23rd Street, NW
(202) 426-6841
Daily, 8:00 A.M.-Midnight

President John F. Kennedy's Grave,
Eternal Flame
Arlington Cemetery

National Zoological Park
3000 Block, Connecticut Avenue, NW
(202) 673-4717
Sept. 16-April 30, Grounds open
8:00 A.M.-6:00 P.M.,
buildings open 9:00 A.M.-4:30 P.M.
May 1-Sept. 15, Grounds open 8:00 A.M.-
8:00 P.M.,
buildings open 9:00 A.M.-6:00 P.M.

Railway cars
Museum of American History
A Smithsonian Museum
Constitution Avenue, between 12th and
14th Streets, NW
(202) 357-2700, 357-2020
Open daily, 10:00 A.M.-5:30 P.M.
Closed Christmas Day

Many of the places listed above are located
within the mall, which is between
Constitution and Independence Avenues
and runs from 3rd street to the Potomac River.

Hours are subject to change. Please call for
current information.

Free information is available from:

Washington Convention and Visitors
Association
1400 Pennsylvania Avenue, NW
Washington, D.C. 20004
(202) 789-7000
Open daily, 9:00 A.M.-5:00 P.M.

Acknowledgments

My thanks to the following people for their help:

Mike Fuller, my resourceful and always dependable lighting assistant; and Bill Geiger, who also assisted.

My office assistant, Robert Hajek, who kept everything organized.

Laura Perry, the sort of editorial assistant every writer dreams about.

Leigh Anne Donahue, Staff Assistant to Senator Joseph R. Biden.

Congressman Tom Downey, his wife Chris Downey, and their daughter Lauren.

Joanne Puglisi, appointments secretary and office manager for Congressman Downey.

John Brademas, George Nicholson, Ole Risom, Tom Jackson, Fred Gerard, Peggy Cafritz, and Kurt Vonnegut, who looked at this book before it went to press and offered valuable suggestions.

Jack Russ, Sergeant at Arms in the House of Representatives; and Sergeant Warren Hurlock, who was especially helpful.

J. Carter Brown, Director at the National Gallery of Art; and Ellen Stanley, Programs Assistant in the Information Office.

At the Washington Cathedral: Nancy S. Montgomery, Communications Director; Linda Freeman; Ann Etches, Manager of the Cathedral's Brass Rubbing Workshop.

Sergeant First Class Woodrow English, Bugler at The Tomb of the Unknown Soldier.

Janet Pawlukiewicz, Office of Education at the National Museum of Natural History. She is the Manager of the Discovery Room.

Margie Gibson, Office of Public Affairs at the National Zoological Park.

Joyce Dall'Acqua, Office of Public Affairs and Museum Services at the National Air and Space Museum; and Tracy Jackson, Office of Protection Services.

Florian H. Thayn, Head, Art and Reference Division, at the Office of the Architect of the Capitol.

At the Bureau of Engraving and Printing: Robert Leuver, Director; Linda Coleman and Leah Akbar, Public Affairs Staff; Donald A. D'Agostino, Office of Security; Delores V. Briscoe and Emma M. Forbes, Currency Examiners.

Alberto Ocampo, Manager of Axxion Copy, who spent many hours with me making color xeroxes from my transparencies while I worked on the layouts for this book.

The always gracious staff at The Four Seasons Hotel.

At Scholastic: Jean Feiwel, Frances Leos, Rose-Ellen Lorber-Termaat, Nancy Pines, Emmeline Hsi, and Diana Hrisinko.

Most of all, I am indebted to the Wilson Family — Matt, Cole, Martha, and Bob. They were a joy to work with and they are a pleasure to know.

j917.53 Krementz, Jill.
K   c.1

A visit to
Washington, D.C

$13.95

DATE			